THE ART OF
OFFENCE
AROUND THE WORLD

LAGOON BOOKS

THE ART OF OFFENCE AROUND THE WORLD

Series Editor: Lucy Dear
Managing Editor: Sarah Wells
Cover and Book Design: Gary Sherwood
Page Layout: Gary Inwood Studio
Thanks to: Eclipse Translations Ltd and
First Edition Translations

Published by:
LAGOON BOOKS
PO BOX 311, KT2 5QW, UK
PO BOX 990676, Boston, MA 02199 USA

ISBN: 190281374X

Printed in Thailand.

Had enough of being unable to get your point across abroad because you can't speak the language? Fume no longer - we have the answer for you!

For the last year our dedicated team of researchers has been traveling the world, testing out thousands of insults to find those which possess truly global offensiveness. They're now resting comfortably in their (hospital) beds, leaving you to reap the fruit of their selfless labors.

In this book you'll find 60 witty and amusing insults guaranteed to cause offence from Madrid to Moscow, Africa to the Arctic Circle. Translations are provided into French, German, Spanish, Italian and Russian - so wherever you are, whatever the occasion, if someone deserves abuse, you'll be ready and able to deliver it.

So what are you waiting for? Pack this book in your bag, pick up a plane ticket and head for the airport. The world is full of foreigners who have the cheek not to speak English. Insult them in their own language, and watch their faces light up. Just be prepared to duck immediately afterwards!

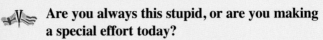

Are you always this stupid, or are you making a special effort today?

Bist du immer so dumm, oder strengst du dich heute ganz besonders an?

¿Eres siempre así de estúpido o estás haciendo hoy un esfuerzo especial?

T'es toujours aussi con ou tu le fais exprès?

Ты всегда такой глупый, или сегодня ты особенно стараешься?

Sci sempre così stupido oppure oggi ti stai impegnando particolarmente?

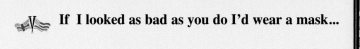

If I looked as bad as you do I'd wear a mask...

Wenn ich so hässlich wäre wie du, würde ich das Haus nicht ohne Maske verlassen!

Si yo tuviese esa cara me pondría una careta...

Si j'étais aussi moche que toi, je me cacherais...

Если бы я выглядел(а) так же ужасно как ты, я бы носил(а) маску.

Se fossi brutto come te mi metterei una maschera...

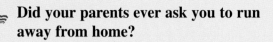 **Did your parents ever ask you to run away from home?**

Haben dich deine Eltern eigentlich nie gebeten, von daheim wegzulaufen?

¿Nunca te han pedido tus padres que te escapes de casa?

Tes parents ne t'ont jamais demandé de partir très loin de la maison?

Тебя родители просили когда-нибудь убежать из дома?

I tuoi genitori ti hanno mai chiesto di scappare di casa?

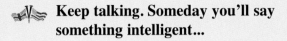 **Keep talking. Someday you'll say something intelligent...**

Rede nur weiter - eines Tages wirst du auch etwas Intelligentes sagen!

Sigue hablando, quizá algún día digas algo inteligente...

Continue de parler, un jour tu finiras par dire quelque chose d'intelligent...

Продолжай говорить, когда-нибудь ты скажешь что-нибудь умное.

Continua a parlare, un giorno o l'altro dirai qualcosa di intelligente...

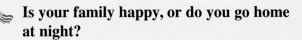 **Is your family happy, or do you go home at night?**

Hat deine Familie Glück, oder gehst du heute Nacht heim?

¿Tu familia es feliz, o sigues yendo a casa todas las noches?

Ta famille n'a pas honte ou tu ne rentres que le soir...

В твоей семье сегодня царит счастье или ты вечером идешь домой?

La tua famiglia è felice oppure torni a casa la sera?

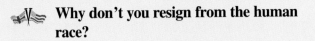 **Why don't you resign from the human race?**

Warum steigst du dich nicht aus der Menschenrasse aus?

¿Por qué no dimites de la raza humana?

Pourquoi tu n'abandonnes pas ta place dans la race humaine?

Почему бы тебе не покинуть человеческую расу?

Perché non ti dimetti dalla razza umana?

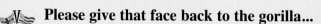 **Please give that face back to the gorilla...**

Gib diese Visage bitte wieder dem Gorilla
zurück...

Devuélvele inmediatemente la cara al gorila...

Sois gentil, rends cette gueule de gorille à son
propriétaire...

Пожалуйста, верни свое лицо горилле.

Per favore, restituisci la faccia al gorilla...

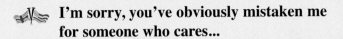 **I'm sorry, you've obviously mistaken me for someone who cares...**

Entschuldige, offenbar verwechselst du mich mit jemand, der an dir Interesse hat...

Lo siento, debes haberme confundido con alguien comprensivo...

Désolé, apparemment tu dois me prendre pour quelqu'un qui s'intéresse à toi...

Извините, вы наверное перепутали меня с тем, кому вы не безразличны.

Mi spiace, mi stai sicuramente confondendo con qualcuno a cui interessi...

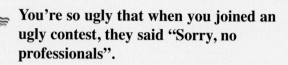 **You're so ugly that when you joined an ugly contest, they said "Sorry, no professionals".**

Du bist so hässlich - wenn du an einem Hässlichkeitswettbewerb teilnehmen wolltest, hieße es: „Sorry, nur für Amateure".

Eres tan feo que te presentaste concurso de feos y te dijeron "lo sentimos, pero no se admiten profesionales".

Tu es tellement moche que si tu te présentes à un concours de laideur, ils te renverront en disant : « Désolé, ici il n'y a que des amateurs ».

Ты настолько безобразен, что если бы ты принял участие в конкурсе уродов, тебе бы сказали: «Извините, профессионалам нельзя».

Sei così brutto che se partecipassi a un concorso di bruttezza di direbbero "Mi spiace, niente professionisti".

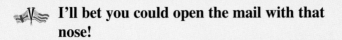 **I'll bet you could open the mail with that nose!**

Ich wette, mit diesem Zinken kannst du Briefe öffnen!

¡Seguro que con esa nariz puedes abrir el correo!

Avec un nez comme le tien, je suis sûr que tu pourrais ouvrir ton courrier!

Держу пари, ты откроешь конверт своим носом!

Scommetto che con quel naso puoi aprire la posta!

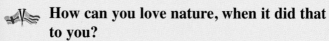 **How can you love nature, when it did that to you?**

Wie kannst du die Natur lieben, wenn sie dir das angetan hat?

¿Cómo puedes amar la naturaleza, después de lo que te ha hecho?

Comment peux-tu aimer la nature, après ce qu'elle t'a fait?

Как ты можешь любить природу, после того как она такое с тобой сотворила?

Come puoi amare la natura quando ti ha fatto questo brutto scherzo?

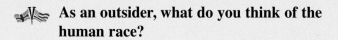 **As an outsider, what do you think of the human race?**

Was sagst du als Außenstehender zur menschlichen Rasse?

Tú que la ves desde fuera, ¿qué te parece la raza humana?

En tant qu'élément extérieur, que penses-tu de l'humanité?

Как не относящийся к человеческой расе, что ты думаешь о ней?

In qualità di elemento esterno, che cosa pensi della razza umana?

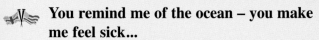 **You remind me of the ocean – you make me feel sick...**

Du erinnerst mich an das Meer – von dir wird mir übel!

Me recuerdas al océano: me das náuseas...

Tu me fais penser à la mer : tu me donnes envie de vomir...

Ты напоминаешь мне океан, меня от тебя тошнит.

Mi ricordi l'oceano: mi fai venire il mal di mare...

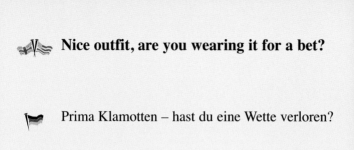

Nice outfit, are you wearing it for a bet?

Prima Klamotten – hast du eine Wette verloren?

Menudo conjuntito, ¿te lo pones por una apuesta?

Pas mal ton accoutrement! C'est pour un pari?

Смешной наряд. Ты что поспорил с кем-то, что будешь это носить?

Bel vestito, lo indossi per scommessa?

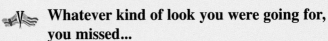 **Whatever kind of look you were going for, you missed...**

Ich weiß zwar nicht, welcher Look dir vorschwebte, aber du liegst definitiv daneben...

Fuera cual fuera el look que querías tener, te equivocaste...

Quelque soit le look que tu cherchais à avoir, c'est raté...

Как бы ты не хотел хорошо выглядеть, тебе это еще ни разу не удалось.

Qualsiasi tipo di aspetto volessi avere, non l'hai azzeccato...

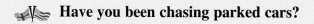 **Have you been chasing parked cars?**

Hast du parkende Autos gejagt?

¿Has estado persiguiendo coches aparcados?

Tu t'es amusé à courir après des voitures garées?

Ты что развлекался, гоняясь за припаркованными машинами?

Stavi inseguendo le macchine parcheggiate?

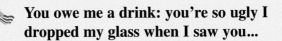 **You owe me a drink: you're so ugly I dropped my glass when I saw you...**

Du schuldest mir einen Drink – du bist so hässlich, dass ich mein Glas fallen ließ, als ich dich sah...

Me debes una copa: eres tan feo que se me cayó la copa al verte...

Tu me dois un coup à boire: tu es tellement laid que j'ai fait tomber mon verre quand je t'ai vu...

Ты должен мне налить: ты настолько отвратителен, что я уронил свой стакан, когда увидел тебя.

Mi devi un drink: sei così brutta che quando ti ho visto mi è caduto il bicchiere dalle mani...

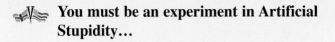 **You must be an experiment in Artificial Stupidity…**

Du warst sicher ein Experiment für künstliche Dummheit...

Tú debes formar parte de un experimento sobre Estupidez Artificial...

Tu fais sûrement partie d'une expérience sur la Connerie Artificielle...

Ты, должно быть - результат эксперимента по искусственной глупости.

Devi essere un esperimento di Stupidità Artificiale…

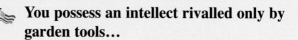

You possess an intellect rivalled only by garden tools…

Dein Intellekt kann sich nur mit Gartenzwergen messen…

Tienes un intelecto sólo igualado por el de una pala...

Ton QI doit avoisiner celui d'un balais...

У тебя интеллект, который может соперничать только с садовым инвентарем.

La tua intelligenza può competere solo con gli attrezzi da giardino…

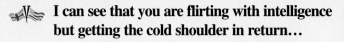 **I can see that you are flirting with intelligence but getting the cold shoulder in return...**

Ich sehe schon, du flirtest mit der Intelligenz, aber sie zeigt dir nur die kalte Schulter...

Veo que estás flirteando con la inteligencia, pero no te está haciendo mucho caso que digamos...

D'après ce que je vois, tu flirtes avec l'intelligence, mais elle, elle te boude...

Насколько я понимаю, ты флиртуешь с интеллектом, но ничего не получаешь взамен.

Vedo che stai flirtando con l'Intelligenza ma lei ti ignora...

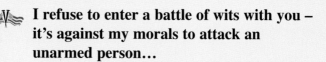 **I refuse to enter a battle of wits with you – it's against my morals to attack an unarmed person…**

Mit dir werde ich meinen Verstand nicht messen – es verstößt nämlich gegen meine Moral, mit Wehrlosen zu kämpfen...

Me niego a entablar una batalla de ingenio contigo: va contra mis principios atacar a alguien desarmado...

Je refuse d'entamer une bataille de mots d'esprit avec toi : c'est contre mes principes d'attaquer une personne désarmée...

Я не буду с вами соревноваться в уме, потому что нападать на безоружного - против моих правил.

Mi rifiuto di partecipare a una gara di intelligenza con te, è contro la mia morale attaccare una persona disarmata...

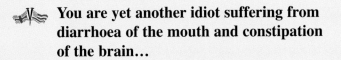 **You are yet another idiot suffering from diarrhoea of the mouth and constipation of the brain...**

Du bist einer dieser Idioten, die an verbalem Durchfall und Gehirnverstopfung leiden...

No eres más que otro idiota que padece diarrea oral y estreñimiento cerebral...

Tu dois encore être un de ces idiots qui souffre de diarrhée verbale et de constipation intellectuelle...

Вы еще один идиот, страдающий от словесного поноса и интеллектуального запора.

Sei un altro idiota che soffre di diarrea della bocca e stitichezza del cervello...

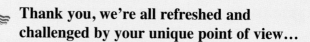 **Thank you, we're all refreshed and challenged by your unique point of view...**

Danke, es war erfrischend und reizvoll für uns alle, deinen wahrhaft einzigartigen Standpunkt zu hören...

Gracias, tu punto de vista único es un soplo de aire fresco para todos...

Merci beaucoup, nous voilà tous requinqués et stimulés par ton point de vue unique....

Большое спасибо, мы все очень заинтригованы вашей уникальной точкой зрения.

Grazie, siamo tutti sollevati e stimolati dal tuo originale punto di vista...

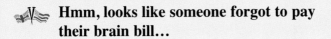

Hmm, looks like someone forgot to pay their brain bill...

Hey, sieht ganz so aus, als hätte jemand vergessen, seine Rechnung ohne den IQ-Wirt gemacht...

Vaya, parece que a alguien se le olvidó pagar la factura de su cerebro...

Oh Oh, on dirait que quelqu'un a oublié de payer la facture pour son cerveau...

Кажется кто-то забыл заплатить по счету за свои мозги.

Hmm, sembra che qualcuno abbia dimenticato di pagare la bolletta del proprio cervello…

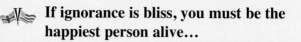 **If ignorance is bliss, you must be the happiest person alive…**

Wenn Unwissenheit selig macht, bist du bestimmt der glücklichste Mensch der Welt…

Si la ignorancia da la felicidad, debes de ser la persona más feliz del mundo…

Heureux sont les pauvres d'esprit ! Mais alors, tu dois être la personne la plus heureuse du monde…

Если невежество - это счастье, то вы, должно быть, самый счастливый человек на свете.

Se l'ignoranza è beatitudine, tu devi essere la persona più felice del mondo…

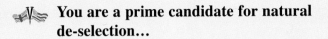 **You are a prime candidate for natural de-selection…**

Du bist der heißeste Anwärter auf natürliche Auslese…

Eres el candidato ideal para quedar eliminado de la selección natural…

Tu dois être un candidat de premier choix à l'exclusion naturelle…

Вы - первый кандидат на естественную деселекцию.

Sei il candidato numero uno alla de-selezione naturale…

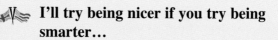 **I'll try being nicer if you try being smarter...**

OK, ich werde versuchen, netter zu sein - wenn du dich bemühst, intelligenter zu sein...

Intentaré ser más amable si tú intentas espabilarte un poco...

J'essayerai d'être plus sympa si tu essaies d'être plus intelligent...

Постараюсь быть повежливей, если вы постараетесь быть поумнее...

Cercherò di essere più gentile se tu cercherai di essere più sveglio...

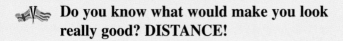 **Do you know what would make you look really good? DISTANCE!**

Weißt du, was dich wirklich gut aussehen ließe? ENTFERNUNG!

¿Sabes lo que te sentaría muy bien? ¡LA DISTANCIA!

Tu sais quelle est la seule chose qui te donnerait vraiment un air bien? LA DISTANCE!

Знаешь, что поможет тебе хорошо выглядеть? РАССТОЯНИЕ!

Sai qual è l'unica cosa che potrebbe farti sembrare veramente bello? La DISTANZA!

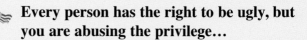 **Every person has the right to be ugly, but you are abusing the privilege…**

Jeder Mensch hat das Recht, hässlich zu sein – aber du missbrauchst dieses Privileg...

Todo el mundo tiene derecho a ser feo, pero tu estás abusando...

Tout le monde a le droit d'être laid, mais toi, tu abuses du privilège...

Каждый имеет право быть безобразным, но вы этим правом злоупотребляете.

Tutti hanno il diritto di essere brutti, ma tu ne stai abusando…

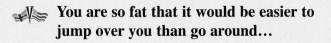 **You are so fat that it would be easier to jump over you than go around...**

Du bist so fett, dass es wohl einfacher ist, über dich zu springen, als um dich herum zu gehen...

Estás tan gordo que es más fácil saltarte que rodearte...

Tu es tellement gros qu'il serait plus facile de sauter par-dessus ta tête que de te contourner...

Ты такой толстый, что мне легче будет перепрыгнуть тебя, чем обойти.

Sei così grasso che sarebbe più semplice scavalcarti che girarti intorno...

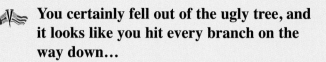 **You certainly fell out of the ugly tree, and it looks like you hit every branch on the way down...**

Du siehst so aus, als wärest du vom Baum der Hässlichkeit gefallen – und beim Sturz hast du jeden einzelnen Ast gestreift...

Desde luego que te has caído del árbol de la fealdad, y parece que has tropezado con cada rama...

Tu es sûrement tombé de l'arbre de la laideur, et apparemment, tu as dû te cogner à toutes les branches avant d'atterrir sur le sol...

Похоже ты свалился с кривого дерева и, по всей видимости, падая, ударялся о каждую ветку.

Sei sicuramente caduto dall' Albero della Brutezza e sembra che cadendo tu abbia colpito ogni singolo ramo...

I'd describe you as dark and handsome: when it's dark, you're handsome...

Ich würde dich als dunkel und gut aussehend beschreiben – wenn es dunkel ist, siehst du gut aus...

Te describiría con dos palabras: oscuridad y atractivo. Sólo en la oscuridad eres atractivo...

Si je devais te décrire en deux mots, je dirais «nuit» et «beau». Eh oui, il n'y a que quand il fait nuit que tu es beau...

Я бы назвала тебя темным и красивым: ты красив, когда темно.

Ti descriverei utilizzando due parole, scuro e attraente: quando è scuro sei attraente...

 **Don't you need a license to be that ugly?**

Braucht man eigentlich einen Waffenschein für so viel Hässlichkeit?

¿No se necesita un permiso especial para ser tan feo?

T'as un permis pour être aussi moche?

А разве не нужно разрешение, чтобы быть таким безобразным?

Non hai bisogno di un permesso per essere così brutto?

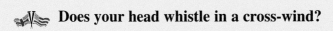 **Does your head whistle in a cross-wind?**

Pfeift dein Kopf bei Gegenwind?

¿Te silba la cabeza cuando sopla el viento de lado?

Et quand le vent vient de travers, ta tête siffle?

У тебя в голове свистит, когда дует ветер?

La tua testa fischia quando il vento soffia di traverso?

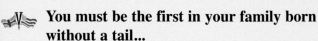 **You must be the first in your family born without a tail...**

Du bist wohl die erste Gestalt in deiner Familie die ohne Schwanz geboren wurde...

Seguro que eres el primero de tu familia que nace sin rabo...

Tu dois certainement être la première dans ta famille à être née sans queue...

Ты, должно быть, первый в семье, кто родился без хвоста.

Devi essere l'unico in famiglia a non avere la coda…

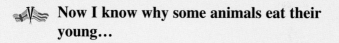

Now I know why some animals eat their young…

Jetzt verstehe ich, warum manche Tiere ihre Jungen fressen…

Ahora comprendo por qué algunos animales devoran a sus crías...

Maintenant je sais pourquoi certains animaux mangent leurs petits...

Теперь понимаю, почему некоторые животные едят своих детей.

Adesso capisco perché alcuni animali mangiano i propri piccoli…

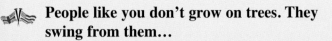 **People like you don't grow on trees. They swing from them...**

Leute wie du wachsen nicht auf Bäumen – sie schwingen sich vielmehr von Ast zu Ast...

La gente como tú no crece en los árboles. Se columpian en ellos...

Les gens comme toi ne poussent pas sur les arbres. Ils en tombent...

Люди вроде тебя на деревьях не растут, они по ним прыгают.

Le persone come te non si trovano mica sugli alberi, cadono dagli alberi...

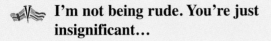 **I'm not being rude. You're just insignificant…**

Ich bin nicht unhöflich. Du bist einfach zu unwichtig…

No es que sea grosero. Es que eres insignificante…

Mais je ne suis pas grossier. Tu es tellement insignifiant…

Я не грублю. Ты просто незаметный.

Non sono scortese, sei tu che sei semplicemente insignificante…

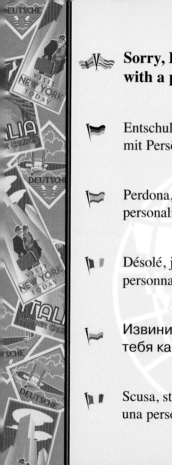

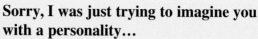 **Sorry, I was just trying to imagine you with a personality...**

Entschuldige, ich habe gerade versucht, dich mir mit Persönlichkeit vorzustellen...

Perdona, es que estaba imaginándote con algo de personalidad...

Désolé, j'essayais juste de t'imaginer avec une personnalité...

Извини, я просто пытался представить тебя как личность.

Scusa, stavo solo cercando di immaginarti con una personalità…

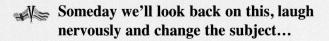

Someday we'll look back on this, laugh nervously and change the subject…

Eines Tages werden wir an diesen Moment zurückdenken, nervös lachen und das Thema wechseln...

Algún día recordaremos esto, nos saldrá una sonrisa nerviosa y cambiaremos de tema...

Un jour, on se rappellera ce moment, on rira nerveusement et on changera de sujet...

Когда-нибудь мы вспомним об этом, нервно посмеемся и сменим тему.

Un giorno ricorderemo tutto ciò, rideremo istericamente e cambieremo argomento…

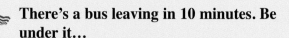 **There's a bus leaving in 10 minutes. Be under it...**

In 10 Minuten fährt ein Bus. Warum legst du dich nicht unter ihn?

Hay un autobús que sale dentro de diez minutos. Ponte debajo...

Il y a un bus qui passe dans dix minutes. Jette-toi dessous...

Через 10 минут отправляется автобус. Пусть он тебя переедет.

C'è un autobus che parte tra 10 minuti. Fatti investire...

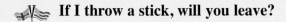 **If I throw a stick, will you leave?**

Würdest du gehen, wenn ich ein Stöckchen werfe?

Si te tiro un palito, ¿correrás a por él y me dejarás tranquilo?

Et si je te lance un bâton, tu vas courir après et te casser enfin?

Если я кину палку, ты побежишь за ней?

Se ti lancio un bastone, vai a riprenderlo e mi lasci in pace?

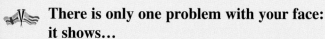 **There is only one problem with your face: it shows...**

Es gibt nur ein Problem mit deinem Gesicht: man kann es sehen...

Tu cara sólo tiene un problema. Se ve demasiado...

Le seul problème avec ta gueule, c'est qu'elle est très voyante...

У тебя одна проблема с лицом – его видно.

La tua faccia ha solo un problema, si vede...

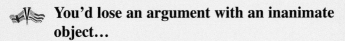

You'd lose an argument with an inanimate object…

Du würdest sogar eine Diskussion mit einem leblosen Gegenstand verlieren...

Tú discutes con una piedra y pierdes...

Tu serais capable d'avoir tort dans une discussion avec un mur...

Ты проспоришь неодушевленному предмету.

In una lite, riusciresti a perdere anche con un muro…

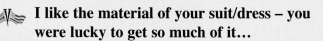 **I like the material of your suit/dress – you were lucky to get so much of it…**

Mir gefällt der Stoff von deinem Kleid/deinem Anzug. Du hattest wirklich Glück, so viel davon zu bekommen...

Me encanta la tela de tu vestido / traje. Tienes suerte de haber conseguido tanta...

J'aime bien le tissu de ta veste / ta robe... Tu as de la chance d'en avoir eu une si grande quantité...

Мне нравится материал твоего костюма/платья – тебе повезло отхватить его так много.

Mi piace il tessuto del tuo vestito, sei stato fortunato/a a trovarne così tanto…

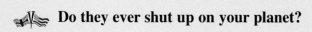 **Do they ever shut up on your planet?**

Hält man auf deinem Planeten eigentlich nie die Klappe?

Es que nunca os calláis en vuestro planeta?

Est-ce qu'il leur arrive parfois de la fermer, sur ta planète?

На твоей планете хоть когда-нибудь замолкают?

Sul tuo pianeta non stanno mai zitti?

 **Have a nice day… somewhere else…**

Ich wünsche dir noch einen schönen Tag …
irgendwo anders…

Que tengas un buen día... en alguna otra parte...

Passe une bonne journée… loin d'ici…

Хорошо проведи этот день…где-нибудь
еще.

Ti auguro una buona giornata… da un'altra
parte…

I didn't know the circus was in town...

Ich wusste gar nicht, dass der Zirkus wieder in der Stadt ist...

No sabía que hubiera llegado el circo a la ciudad...

Je ne savais pas qu'il y avait un cirque en ville...

Я не знал, что в город приехал цирк.

Non sapevo che il circo fosse in città…

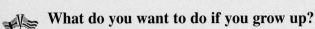

What do you want to do if you grow up?

Was möchtest du machen, falls du je erwachsen wirst?

¿Que querrías ser si crecieras algún día?

Qu'est-ce que tu voudrais faire plus tard, si tu grandissais?

Чем займешься, если вырастешь?

Cosa vuoi fare se diventerai grande?

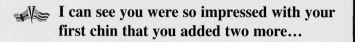

I can see you were so impressed with your first chin that you added two more...

Wie ich sehe, warst du von deinem ersten Kinn so begeistert, dass du es gleich verdreifacht hast...

Veo que te gustó tanto tu primera papada que has añadido un par de ellas...

D'après ce que je vois, tu as été tellement impressionné par ton premier menton que tu en as ajouté deux de plus...

Я знаю, что ты так восхищался своим подбородком, что добавил еще два.

Noto che eri così soddisfatto del tuo primo mento che hai deciso di aggiungerne altri due...

I'm not going deaf – I am ignoring you...

Nein, ich bin nicht plötzlich taub – ich ignoriere dich einfach...

No estoy sordo; es que no te hago ningún caso...

Je ne suis pas sourd, je t'ignore...

Я не глухой, я тебя игнорирую.

Non sto diventando sordo, ti sto ignorando...

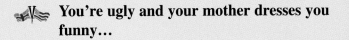 **You're ugly and your mother dresses you funny...**

Du bist hässlich, und deine Mutter zieht dir komische Kleider an...

De por sí ya eres feo, pero encima tu madre te viste muy mal...

Pauvre gars / fille, tu es déjà moche et en plus ta mère t'habille comme un sac...

Ты такой страшный, и твоя мама так смешно тебя одевает.

Sei già brutto e per di più tua mamma ti veste in modo buffo...

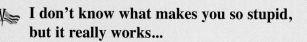 **I don't know what makes you so stupid, but it really works...**

Ich weiss nicht, was dich so blöde macht, aber es klappt wirklich...

No sé qué es lo que te hace tan estúpido, ¡pero funciona!

Je ne sais pas ce qui te rend tellement bête, mais ça marche vraiment...

То, что делает тебя таким глупым, действует хорошо.

Non so cos'è che ti rende cosi stupido, ma funziona!

I bet when you go to the zoo, you have to buy two tickets: one to get in and one to get out…

Ich wette, wenn du in den Zoo gehst, musst du 2 Karten kaufen – eine, um reinzukommen, und die zweite, damit man dich wieder rauslässt...

Seguro que cuando vas al zoo tienes que comprar dos entradas. Una para entrar y otra para salir...

Je parie que quand tu vas au zoo, t'es obligé d'acheter deux billets. Un pour rentrer, et un pour qu'ils te laissent sortir...

Держу пари, что, когда ты идешь в зоопарк, тебе приходится покупать два билета. Один - чтобы войти, второй - чтобы выйти.

Scommetto che quando vai allo zoo devi comprare due biglietti: uno per entrare e uno per uscire…

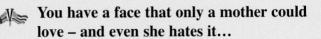 **You have a face that only a mother could love – and even she hates it…**

Du hast ein Gesicht, das nur eine Mutter lieben könnte – und sogar sie hasst es…

Tienes una cara que sólo puede gustarle a una madre; y la tuya la odia...

Tu as une tronche que seule une mère peut aimer ; et encore, elle doit faire semblant...

У тебя лицо такое, что только мать его может любить, но даже она его ненавидит.

Hai una faccia che solo a tua madre potrebbe piacere e comunque pure lei non la sopporta…

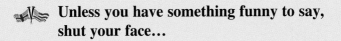 **Unless you have something funny to say, shut your face...**

Falls du nichts Komisches zu sagen hast, halte ganz einfach die Klappe...

A menos que tengas algo gracioso que decir, cierra la boca...

Si tu as quelque chose de drôle à dire, vas-y ; sinon ferme-la...

Если рассмешить нечем, заткнись.

A meno che tu non abbia qualcosa di divertente da dire, chiudi il becco...

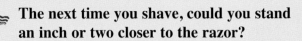 **The next time you shave, could you stand an inch or two closer to the razor?**

Wenn du dich das nächste Mal rasierst, könntest du bitte etwas näher an die Klinge treten?

¿La próxima vez que te afeites, acércate un poco a la maquinilla?

La prochaine fois que tu te rases, approche-toi un peu plus près du rasoir?

В следующий раз, когда будешь бриться, пододвинься на пару сантиметров поближе к бритве?

La prossima volta che ti fai la barba, potresti stare un po' più vicino al rasoio?

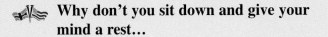

Why don't you sit down and give your mind a rest...

Warum setzt du dich nicht einfach hin und gönnst deinem Hirn eine kleine Pause...

Porqué no te sientas y descansas un poco la mente...

Tu ferais mieux de t'asseoir et de laisser reposer ta tête...

Присядь дай мозгам отдохнуть.

Perché non ti siedi e fai riposare il cervello…

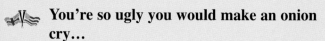 You're so ugly you would make an onion cry...

Du bist so hässlich, dass du eine Zwiebel zum Heulen bringst...

Eres tan feo que harías llorar a las cebollas...

Tu es tellement laid que tu ferais pleurer un oignon...

Такой урод, как ты даже лук заставит плакать.

Sei così brutto che faresti piangere una cipolla...

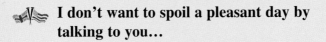 **I don't want to spoil a pleasant day by talking to you...**

Ich möchte diesen angenehmen Tag nicht dadurch verderben, dass ich mich mit dir unterhalte...

No quiero estropearme un día tan maravilloso hablando contigo...

Je n'ai pas envie de gâcher une si belle journée en parlant avec toi...

Не хочу портить приятный день, разговаривая с тобой.

Non voglio rovinare una bella giornata parlando con te…